The Shakespeare Library

Twelfth Night

WENDY GREENHILL

HEAD OF EDUCATION

ROYAL SHAKESPEARE COMPANY

and

PAUL WIGNALL

Heinemann LIBRARY

First published in Great Britain by Heinemann Library
Halley Court, Jordan Hill, Oxford OX2 8EJ
a division of Reed Educational & Professional Publishing Ltd

OXFORD FLORENCE PRAGUE MADRID ATHENS
MELBOURNE AUCKLAND KUALA LUMPUR SINGAPORE TOKYO
IBADAN NAIROBI KAMPALA JOHANNESBURG GABORONE
PORTSMOUTH NH (USA) CHICAGO MEXICO CITY SAO PAULO

© Reed Educational & Professional Publishing 1997

Designed by Ken Vail Graphic Design, Cambridge
Printed in Great Britain by Bath Press Colourbooks, Glasgow

01 00 99 98 97
10 9 8 7 6 5 4 3 2 1

British Library Cataloguing in Publication Data

Greenhill, Wendy
Twelfth Night – (The Shakespeare library)
1. Shakespeare, William, 1564-1616. Twelfth Night – Juvenile literature
2. English drama – Early Modern and Elizabethan, 1500–1600
– History and criticism – Juvenile literature
I.Title II.Wignall, Paul
822.3'3

ISBN 0 431 07537 9

Acknowledgements
The authors and publishers would like to thank the following for permission
to reproduce photographs and other illustrative material:

The Ancient Art and Architecture Collection, page 17;
The Bodleian Library, page 5;
The Honourable Society of the Middle Temple, page 4;
The Performing Arts Library (Clive Barda), page 25;
Donald Cooper: Photostage, cover & pages 7, 26, 27 (right), 28, 31;
The Shakespeare Centre Library: Stratford-upon-Avon,
pages 6, 8, 10 ,12, 13, 15, 23, 24, 27 (left), 28, 30;
The University of Michigan, page 23;
The Victoria and Albert Museum, pages 19, 21.

The cover shows Desmond Barrit as Malvolio in the 1994 Royal Shakespeare Company production.

Our thanks to Jean Black for her comments in the preparation of this book.

In preparing this book, the authors have used the text of *Twelfth Night* from
William Shakespeare The Complete Works, Clarendon Press, Oxford 1986

Names in **bold** in the text are characters in the play.

CONTENTS

INTRODUCTION

When William Shakespeare wrote *Twelfth Night*, probably in 1601, he was enjoying huge success as an actor and playwright in the theatre in London. He was one of the leaders of the company of actors to which he belonged, The Lord Chamberlain's Men, and his plays were drawing large audiences to The Globe, their new theatre on the south bank of the Thames.

All companies of actors needed the support and protection of powerful noblemen to prevent them from being arrested as vagabonds (homeless beggars). Shakespeare and his fellow actors had an important patron in the Lord Chamberlain. He was one of Queen Elizabeth I's ministers and his duties included organizing the entertainments for the Queen and her guests. The Lord Chamberlain's Men were required to perform at court several times a year.

This earned them good money and immense prestige. Shakespeare, who as a young man had come to London from the small market town of Stratford-upon-Avon in Warwickshire, had made his mark.

FEASTING AND FOOLING

The full title of the play – *Twelfth Night, Or What You Will* – suggests something lighthearted. The twelfth and last day of Christmas, 6 January, was celebrated riotously. The day of feasting and fooling was often led by a 'Lord of Misrule', someone chosen to create disorder, and dramatic entertainment, music and dancing were all part of the fun.

The Lord Chamberlain's Men performed at court on Twelfth Night 1601 as part of the Queen's lavish Christmas celebrations. It is just possible that the play they presented was *Twelfth Night*. More likely, Shakespeare wrote his play after that event, perhaps partly inspired by it.

The Hall of the Middle Temple, one of the Inns of Court in London, where *Twelfth Night* was performed on 2 February 1602.

AN EARLY PERFORMANCE

It is known that *Twelfth Night* was performed in the Hall of the Middle Temple in London on 2 February 1602 and this may have been its first performance. The Middle Temple was one of the Inns of Court, where young men training to be lawyers lived and studied. One of them, John Massingham, wrote an account of the performance in his diary:

> **'... at our feast we had a play called** Twelfth Night Or What You Will. **A good practice to make the steward believe his lady was in love with him ...'**

SOURCES

Shakespeare was never shy about using other people's work as the basis for his plays. For *Twelfth Night* he used much of the story of a romantic tale called *Farewell to Militarie Profession* published by Barnaby Riche in 1581. This was itself based on an Italian play, *Gl'Ingannati* ('The Deceptions'), performed in 1531. What is interesting are the additions Shakespeare made to these originals. He sets his play in Illyria – now Croatia – although he turns it into an imaginary country, at once strange, and yet with many features of his own London. For his play, Shakespeare added four new characters: **Sir Toby Belch**, **Sir Andrew Aguecheek**, **Malvolio** and **Feste**. They not only add much to the comedy of the play, they also extend the range of its moods.

Twelfth Night is a very funny play, but it has elements of seriousness which constantly remind the audience that young people grow old and die, that though we may laugh, tears are never far away, and that the search for love can be tender, or painful, or even downright foolish.

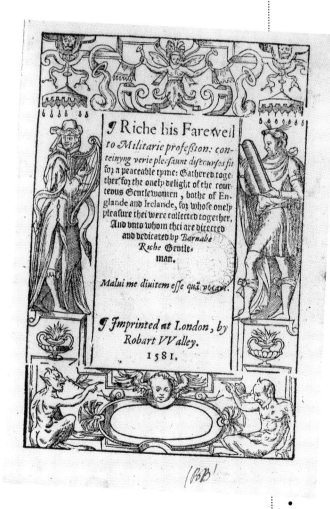

The frontispiece to Barnaby Riche's romantic tale, *Farewell to Militarie Profession*, a source for much of the plot of *Twelfth Night*.

THE CHARACTERS

Orsino is the Duke of Illyria. He is courting Olivia, a countess.

Valentine and **Curio** are courtiers – gentlemen who attend Orsino.

Viola is a young lady who lands on Illyria when her ship is wrecked in a storm at sea. She disguises herself as a boy, **Cesario**, and serves Orsino.

There is a **Sea Captain** who helps Viola.

Sebastian is Viola's twin brother.

Antonio is another sea captain and a friend of Sebastian.

Olivia is a countess, living in Illyria.

Maria is Olivia's gentlewoman, her servant and companion.

Sir Toby Belch is Olivia's uncle, living in her household.

Sir Andrew Aguecheek is a companion of Sir Toby. He has come to Olivia's house in the hope that she will agree to marry him.

Malvolio is Olivia's steward. He is her chief servant with responsibility for her household.

Fabian is another servant in Olivia's household.

Feste is Olivia's fool or jester – her household entertainer.

There is also a **Priest** and other **servants**, **officers**, **musicians** and **sailors**.

'With hey, ho, the wind and the rain.'
An early twentieth century drawing of Feste by W. Heath Robinson.

Freddie Jones as Malvolio
at the Royal Shakespeare
Company (RSC), 1991.

WHAT HAPPENS
IN THE PLAY

Orsino is in love, but **Olivia**, the woman he loves, will have nothing to do with him. **Curio**, a gentleman in Orsino's court, tries in vain to get the duke to think of other things. Then **Valentine**, another of the duke's attendants, comes with a message from Olivia. She is still rejecting Orsino; she is in mourning for her brother who has died and refuses to think of anything else.

Meanwhile, a storm off the coast of Illyria has wrecked a ship carrying **Viola**, a young woman, and her twin brother **Sebastian**. Viola has been saved by a **Sea Captain** but they fear that Sebastian has been drowned.

The captain tells Viola where they are, and about the situation between Orsino and Olivia. Viola has heard of Orsino before from her father. Alone now, and in a strange country, she decides the best thing will be to dress as a young man and try to get employment at Orsino's court:

'What else may hap [happen] to time I will commit.'

'What country, friends, is this?' Cherie Lunghi as Viola and the Sea Captain from the RSC's 1979 production.

At Olivia's house **Sir Toby Belch**, her hard-drinking uncle, is being given a warning by **Maria**, the countess's lady-in-waiting. She has heard Olivia making unfavourable comments about Sir Toby's bad habits, and about **Sir Andrew Aguecheek**, whom Sir Toby has brought into the household. If they don't behave themselves, Olivia is likely to throw them out.

A BATTLE OF WITS

Sir Toby protests that Sir Andrew is brave, clever and rich. Maria thinks he's a fool. Sir Andrew comes in, and it's clear at once that Maria is right: she runs rings round him in a battle of wits. When she has left them, Sir Toby tells Sir Andrew that he needs a drink to improve his wits. But Aguecheek is fed up: Olivia wants nothing to do with him; he might as well go home. However, the promise of a good time drinking and dancing makes him quickly change his mind.

VIOLA BECOMES CESARIO

Viola has dressed herself as a boy and become an attendant at Orsino's court, calling herself **Cesario**. Orsino is so taken with the new arrival that he decides to send Cesario to Olivia in the hope that this new messenger will make the countess change her mind. Viola agrees to go but with some doubts: she is already falling in love with Orsino herself:

> **'Whoe'er I woo, myself would be his wife.'**

FESTE AND MALVOLIO

At Olivia's house, **Feste**, her fool, has been missing. Now he has turned up, Maria tells him he's in trouble. But his wit turns Maria's anger into sympathy as Olivia and **Malvolio** arrive. Olivia is still angry with Feste and tells him to go away, but Feste boldly turns this on her, calling her a fool. She is annoyed but fascinated – what does Feste mean? He asks for permission to show her. He asks why she is in mourning. 'For my brother's death,' she replies. He must be in hell, says Feste. Olivia retorts that he's in heaven. 'The more fool … to mourn for your brother's soul, being in heaven.' So Feste has both comforted and amused Olivia.

Malvolio is not so easily appeased – he doesn't like Feste's wit. Olivia accuses him of being 'sick of self-love' (so pompous and sure of himself that he can't enjoy humour) and praises Feste. As an 'allowed fool' it's his job to speak the truth and to make fun, however hard that might be to accept; it can only be for the good in the end.

Maria announces another messenger, arrived from Orsino. Olivia tells Malvolio to send him away and he's hardly gone before Sir Toby arrives. Although it's still morning, he's very drunk. He too has come to tell Olivia that 'a gentleman' is at the gate. Sir Toby wanders away, followed by Maria.

OLIVIA AND CESARIO

All Malvolio's efforts to send the messenger away have failed:

> **'He'll speak with you, will you or no.'**

Malvolio describes the young man – he's obviously handsome and Olivia wants to know more. She calls for Maria and sends Malvolio off to fetch Orsino's man. Olivia and Maria decide to play a trick on the youth. They both put veils over their faces and when Cesario comes in he has to ask which is Olivia. At first they won't tell him, but he refuses to give his message to anyone but Olivia. Olivia tells Cesario he must leave.

Maria tries to take him away, but Cesario refuses to go, insisting on giving his message from the duke. Olivia relents – Cesario is, after all, a handsome young man. Maria is sent away and Cesario begins. He soon stops, though, and asks to see Olivia's face. She lifts her veil, proud of her beauty. 'Is't not well done?' she asks, meaning 'Am I not beautiful?' Viola is taken aback. Olivia is indeed beautiful, and she is Viola's rival for Orsino. So Viola, in her disguise as Cesario, answers wittily and cuttingly:

> **'Excellently done, if God did all.'**

In other words, 'You certainly seem to be beautiful, but how much of that is your make-up!'

Antonio shows himself a true friend to Sebastian. Stratford, 1993.

Viola/Cesario delivers the message from Orsino and Olivia is hooked – not by the message but by the messenger. She asks Cesario to come back again when she will give an answer to the duke. Cesario goes. Now the countess calls for Malvolio and hands him a ring. She says it is from Orsino, and must be returned to Cesario; in fact, she's giving it to Cesario as a gift – Olivia has fallen in love.

SEBASTIAN

Back at the coast, another young person has been washed ashore after the shipwreck. Sebastian is mourning the loss of his twin sister, whom he believes to have been drowned in the wreck from which he has been saved. Sebastian is making for Orsino's court. His companion, **Antonio**, knows of the place. Although he is a wanted man there, following a recent war between his country and Orsino's, Antonio decides to follow Sebastian.

MALVOLIO, CESARIO AND THE RING

Meanwhile, Malvolio catches up with Cesario and tries to hand over the ring, which he believes to be a gift from Orsino which Olivia has rejected. Viola/Cesario is bewildered – she didn't give Olivia a ring from Orsino. However, she covers up for Olivia by saying that the countess actually took the ring off her. When Cesario refuses to take the ring, Malvolio drops it on the ground in front of Cesario and walks away.

Alone now, Viola/Cesario reflects on the situation. She is beginning to see the truth and to understand what Olivia is doing:

'She loves me ... Poor thing, she were better love a dream.'

Viola realizes that the game she is playing has become serious:

'My master loves her dearly; And I, poor monster, fond as much on him; And she, mistaken, seems to dote on me ... O time, thou must untangle this, not I! It is too hard a knot for me t'untie.''

CAKES AND ALE

It is late at night at Olivia's house. Sir Toby and Sir Andrew have been out drinking and come in, noisy and drunk. Sir Toby shouts for more wine. Feste comes to them and they persuade him to sing for them. Feste sings a sad love song: 'O Mistress Mine'. It seems to sadden them, and Belch shouts for a jollier song. All three of them are soon singing at the tops of their voices. They wake Maria who tries, completely unsuccessfully, to calm them down. They have also woken Malvolio, who attempts to bring them to order, but they mock him and refuse to be quiet. Sir Toby turns on Malvolio:

'Dost thou think, because thou art virtuous, there shall be no more cakes and ale?'

MARIA'S PLOT

Malvolio leaves, threatening to tell Olivia what's been going on. This is the last straw for the revellers and they start to work out a plot to make Malvolio look a fool. Maria says that her handwriting is like Olivia's and she will write a letter to trap Malvolio into an embarrassing situation. Maria may well see Malvolio as her rival in Olivia's household: she seems only too pleased to undermine his position! She goes off to bed while Sir Toby persuades Sir Andrew to join him in another drink.

ORSINO AND CESARIO

Viola/Cesario is back at Orsino's court. Feste is with them (although Olivia's fool, he performs anywhere if he's paid). He sings another sad love song: 'Come away, death'. Then Orsino tells Cesario he's more lovesick than any woman could be.

But Viola makes up a story about her 'sister' who pined away for love. Moved by this, Orsino asks if the girl died. Realizing how close she is to telling Orsino the truth about herself she answers him with a riddle:

**'I am all the daughters of my father's house,
And all the brothers too; and yet I know not ...'**

She quickly changes the subject and asks if she should go to Olivia again.

THE LETTER

Maria has written the letter, pretending it is from Olivia. She brings it to the garden where Belch, Aguecheek and another servant, **Fabian**, are waiting. She throws the letter down and they hide in a box-tree to see what will happen. Malvolio is out walking in the garden, day-dreaming about what life would be like if he were to be married to Olivia.

'My father had a daughter loved a man ...' The lovesick Orsino (Clive Wood) listens to Viola/Cesario (Emma Fielding), at Stratford in 1993.

He sees the letter, picks it up, opens it, and reads. He is sure it is from Olivia and is meant for him. The letter is a riddle which seems to be telling him that Olivia loves him and wants to promote him in his job as steward, and even to marry him.

> **'Some are born great, some achieve greatness, and some have greatness thrust upon 'em.'**

The letter praises yellow stockings worn with garters and tells Malvolio to smile when he is with Olivia. Completely taken in, Malvolio goes off to find some yellow stockings and prepare to meet Olivia – smiling.

After he has gone the plotters celebrate the success of their trick. Maria points out that Olivia actually hates yellow stockings and garters, and if Malvolio smiles, it will only make her more angry.

RIVALS FOR OLIVIA

Cesario is on his way to Olivia's house when he meets Feste again. The fool begs money in exchange for witty remarks. When Feste has gone, Belch and Aguecheek arrive, soon followed by Olivia and Maria. Olivia tells the others to leave her alone with Cesario. When they have gone the countess again rejects Orsino.

Malvolio, played by Emrys James, reads Maria's mischievous letter in the RSC's 1983 production: 'Some are born great, some achieve greatness, and some have greatness thrust upon 'em.'

But she tries to persuade his messenger to come back again. Cesario refuses and leaves.

Sir Andrew, too, has decided to leave: he's sure that Olivia loves Cesario. Toby persuades him that if that is the case, he'd better challenge the young man to a duel. Aguecheek leaves to write the letter of challenge as Maria arrives. She has seen Malvolio – dressed in yellow stockings and garters. He's on his way to Olivia with a smile on his face.

Meanwhile Sebastian and Antonio have arrived at the town near Orsino's court. Antonio explains that he is likely to be arrested if discovered. He asks Sebastian to look after his money and arranges to meet him at the place where they are staying later in the day.

YELLOW STOCKINGS

At Olivia's house, Malvolio appears dressed in yellow stockings with fantastic cross-garters. Olivia is amazed and, when Malvolio seems unable to stop smiling at her, is convinced he has gone mad. She tells Maria, Fabian and Sir Toby to take care of Malvolio but, after she's gone, they just wind Malvolio up even more.

The steward leaves and Sir Andrew arrives with his letter for Cesario. It is a ridiculous challenge and Sir Toby decides to make still more trouble by delivering it in person. Olivia and Cesario approach and when Olivia has gone again, Sir Toby and Fabian tell Cesario that Sir Andrew wants to fight him. They make Aguecheek seem more fierce than he really is and when he returns they tell him that Cesario is a skilful fencer. Much against both their wills, they fight.

MISTAKEN IDENTITY

Almost at once Antonio appears. He mistakes Cesario for Sebastian and defends him. Then officers come to arrest Antonio, who asks Cesario for the money he has lent him. Viola/Cesario is completely mystified and Antonio thinks he has been betrayed by the man he thought was his friend. The officers take Antonio away, but Viola has heard the name of Sebastian – her twin brother!

A little while later Feste sees Sebastian. Thinking he is Cesario, he tells him Olivia has sent for him. Sebastian is confused but when Sir Toby and Sir Andrew appear to resume the quarrel, he draws his sword and beats them. Olivia arrives. She breaks up the fight and declares her love for the young man – thinking it is Cesario – and invites him into her house. Overwhelmed by her beauty, Sebastian follows her.

Malvolio has been locked away because of his 'madness'. Sir Toby and Maria persuade Feste to dress up as a clergyman – Sir Topas – and make fun of the steward. Protesting he is not mad, Malvolio asks for pen and paper to write to Olivia. Feste agrees: he is tired of the joke.

Sebastian comes out of Olivia's house in a lovesick daze. Olivia follows him with a priest. She asks Sebastian to marry her, still thinking he is Cesario. Sebastian agrees.

ALL IS REVEALED

Things move quickly to their climax. Feste arrives with the letter from Malvolio. Orsino and Cesario follow, and then Antonio with the officers. Antonio is trying to explain about Sebastian when Olivia arrives. Seeing Cesario, she calls him 'husband'. The priest confirms it. Orsino turns on Cesario for his falseness but is interrupted by Aguecheek who has been wounded – by the person he thinks is Cesario!

Again Cesario denies all knowledge of what's been going on. Then it happens – Sebastian joins them and the twins are united:

> **'One face, one voice, one habit and two persons!'**

Feste now interrupts to remind them of Malvolio's letter. After she has read it, Olivia sends for the steward. While they are waiting, Orsino realizes he loves Viola, as Cesario has revealed 'himself' to be, and asks her to marry him. She agrees.

Malvolio arrives. The trick is explained but he will not forgive them. He stalks off threatening to get his own back: 'I'll be revenged on the whole pack of you!'

The loves are united: Sebastian and Olivia are married and so, we hear, are Sir Toby and Maria. Viola and Orsino will be married soon. Only Aguecheek is without a partner. But the play ends on a bitter-sweet note. No good thing lasts for ever, Feste sings at the close,

> **'For the rain it raineth every day.'**

The company in the final scenes of the 1983 production at Stratford.

TWELFTH NIGHT...

A t first sight the play looks like a great celebration. It is often funny, with lovely songs, and it seems to end happily with three couples about to embark on marriage. Yet, as so often in Shakespeare's works, the world of the play is much more complex, even disturbing, than first impressions might suggest.

This is a world where characters often doubt their sanity. 'Mad' and 'madness' are words which come up often in the play. They may be used in confused delight, as by **Sebastian**, 'Or am I mad, or else this is a dream.' Or they may be used cruelly, as by **Feste** when, as Sir Topas, he tells **Malvolio** that he is mad. Malvolio clings to his own sense of reality and insists: 'I am as well in my wits as any man in Illyria.'

UNRULY CELEBRATIONS

For the Elizabethans, Twelfth Night was a riotous feast, a blast of high spirits in the middle of winter. The celebration wasn't just eating and drinking. What was usually forbidden was encouraged by a 'Lord of Misrule', a sort of master of ceremonies, often a young boy, chosen to stir up the confusion. **Sir Toby Belch** and **Maria** are like a Lord and Lady of Misrule:

setting up the tricks to cut Malvolio down to size, encouraging the duel between **Sir Andrew** and **Cesario**, and generally encouraging noisy celebration and high jinks.

Even here, Shakespeare asks a darker and more serious question: Maria's letter, seeming to come from **Olivia**, does the trick and makes Malvolio look ridiculous. But then she, Sir Toby and Feste push it further, beyond the boundaries of fun and games. The Sir Topas episode is a cruel punishment of Malvolio, who stops being a figure of fun when he is locked up and left alone in the dark. Feste sees that the joke has got out of hand, and helps Malvolio write a letter to Olivia. Misrule has toppled into cruelty. All the fun and the fooling turn sour. Is Shakespeare asking the audience to consider how close humour can be to nastiness, how narrow the line is between being funny and being cruel?

THE VALUE OF TRUE FRIENDSHIP

Sir Toby's character is also worth questioning. On the surface he is the man who turns ordinary life into a party, who enjoys 'cakes and ale' and shares his own high spirits with everyone around him.

But is he simply a good man having a good time? What about his 'friendship' with Sir Andrew? Aguecheek's money is clearly one of his attractions: 'Send for money, knight.' It is questionable whether Sir Toby knows what being a true friend is about. He sets up the duel with Cesario and then brutally rejects Sir Andrew's affectionate offer of help by calling him insulting names when they have both been wounded by Sebastian.

What a contrast Sir Toby's changeable and often manipulative relationship with Sir Andrew is to that of Antonio with Sebastian. Antonio follows his friend into danger, saves him (so he thinks) in a duel, and is devastated when Cesario (who he thinks is Sebastian) rejects him.

Twelfth Night is a comedy that constantly exposes sadness and pain. This is clear in the character of Feste, the professional clown.

Turning up at Olivia's house at the beginning of the play after a long absence, he joins in the fun but always undercuts it with sad songs. At the end he is left alone to sing again – another hauntingly sad song about the hardness of life. Although Feste is a fool – an 'allowed fool', a professional teller of jokes and singer of songs – he is, in the end, wiser than all the rest, warning that life cannot always be easy and pleasurable.

'Pleasure will be paid one time or another ... The whirligig of time brings in his revenges.'

This painting by the Flemish artist Pieter Bruegel (c.1520–69) is of a peasant wedding. Twelfth Night celebrations would have been very similar.

... OR WHAT YOU WILL

Twelfth Night is a play about desire. It explores the confusions between what people think they want and what they really want. Love and friendship colour the play, but in wildly different moods. It opens with the lovesick **Orsino** moping about **Olivia**. His is a self-conscious obsession with no room for the rest of life. Orsino remains distant, sending messengers to plead for him whilst he acts the tormented lover at home. Since he never sees Olivia, he doesn't know if it is real love or not.

CONTRAST

This contrast between love of oneself and love of somebody else runs through the whole play. Self-love means thinking only about yourself and your feelings, while pretending to be concerned for others. True love means forgetting about yourself and being fully committed to the other person.

Olivia's fixation on the death of her brother suggests a similar personality to Orsino: her mourning is so inward-looking it has lost touch with reality, as **Feste** neatly and wittily shows her. **Viola**, on the other hand, believes her brother to be dead but doesn't turn her love or grief into a pose. She doesn't put on mourning clothes, she puts on boys' clothes.

She is realistic, deciding on a plan for her own survival. Yet her grief is real. She is desperate to remember every detail of the shipwreck, clinging to any faint hope that **Sebastian** might have survived: 'Perchance he is not drowned. What think you, sailors?'

DEEP FRIENDSHIP

Sebastian has not only survived, he has gained a remarkable friend and protector – **Antonio**. There are many deep, loving friendships in Shakespeare's plays and this is probably the most unselfish: a beautiful picture of one man's love for another, even though there is a risk of capture, torture and death. Antonio knows that he is a wanted man in Illyria, so it would be wise to leave as soon as possible. But love overcomes common sense.

Feste's wit jogs Olivia out of her tragic mood. Almost at once she forgets her sadness and her curiosity is aroused by the 'young man' at the gate. She lets Cesario deliver Orsino's latest love speeches and by the time she has heard them she is hopelessly in love with the messenger. But, 'poor lady, she were better love a dream.' Just as the Lord and Lady of Misrule seem to turn things on their head, so love is engaged in the same work.

Both Olivia and Orsino are in love with dreams: neither stops for long enough to ask what substance and reality there is to their feelings.

Aguecheek, too, is hopelessly pursuing Olivia, without ever facing the facts about the pointlessness of his courtship. **Malvolio** is so full of self-love that he allows himself to fantasize about marrying Olivia, and is trapped by **Maria**'s letter into thinking there's a chance that these dreams will come true. But eventually reality hits home: Orsino sees and responds to Viola's love; Olivia marries Sebastian (the male version of Cesario, as it were); Aguecheek leaves, a sadder, but probably no wiser, man. Malvolio stalks off, swearing revenge.

FINDING THE OTHER HALF

Above all, Viola and Sebastian find one another. Here Shakespeare is exploring a very old idea that everyone in the world is searching for their 'other half', which will make them 'whole'.

Viola and Sebastian, the twins, are the most telling example, but Viola and Orsino, Olivia and Sebastian, Sebastian and Antonio, even **Sir Toby** and Maria, show different ways in which two separate beings can come together as a single, loving whole. And so the confusions of *Twelfth Night* come to an end.

Nicholas Hilliard (1547–1619) was a fashionable painter of miniature portraits at the time of Shakespeare. He was court painter to Elizabeth I and James I. *A Youth Leaning Against A Tree Among Roses* shows us the kind of beautiful young man who might have been a courtier, as Viola/Cesario was to Orsino.

THE STAGE HISTORY OF
TWELFTH NIGHT

After the first recorded performance of *Twelfth Night* in 1602, it is almost certain that the play was regularly performed by the King's Men (as Shakespeare's company was renamed after King James I came to the throne in 1603). We know that when King Charles I saw it in 1623, it had been renamed *Malvolio*.

PURITANS

In **Malvolio**, Shakespeare draws a picture of a Puritan, obsessed with rules and regulations, full of his own importance, opposed to fun and games, but ambitious for power. Puritans believed that all men and women were responsible for their own actions before God, and that a strict moral life had no room for idle pleasure. They greatly disliked theatre and Shakespeare's company of actors would have had many disagreements with the Puritan-influenced government of London.

PUBLIC THEATRES CLOSED

Puritanism was the rising force in English life in the years following Shakespeare's death in 1616. Oliver Cromwell, who ruled the country after the execution of King Charles I in 1649, and his Puritan supporters disapproved of public theatres so much that they closed them down.

There were no public performances in London between 1649 and 1660, when the pleasure-loving King Charles II came to the throne and the theatres opened once more. It is not surprising that *Twelfth Night*, the play about love and 'cakes and ale', in which a kill-joy Puritan was punished, was a popular choice. Samuel Pepys, whose famous diary tells us so much about English life at this time, saw it three times, but hated it:

> **'... silly ... one of the weakest plays that ever I saw on stage.'**

Maybe the actors were playing for easy laughs?

ADAPTING SHAKESPEARE'S ORIGINAL

In 1703 there was an adaptation of the play, called *Love Betrayed*, one of several versions of Shakespeare's plays at that time which simplify the originals, adjusting them for changed tastes. During the eighteenth century there were different attitudes towards Malvolio. In 1741, the Irish actor Charles Macklin drew out the sadness of this lonely figure. On the other hand, a critic writing in 1771 described Malvolio as 'that ridiculous composition of stiff impertinence and uncommon conceit.'

The play was frequently staged in the nineteenth century in the fashionable London theatres. There was even an operatic version which was popular for some years. When a play is well known, actors feel a particular challenge to make their mark – to do something different with a role. In 1865 Kate Terry played both **Viola** and **Sebastian**. Later on her sister, Ellen Terry, gave Viola a wistful and resigned air in a production staged by one of the great actor-managers, Sir Henry Irving.

CRITICISM

Critics writing about eighteenth- and nineteenth-century performances were interested in the leading characters and the actors who played them, but sometimes had problems with the play itself.
Dr Samuel Johnson, writing in the middle of the eighteenth century, praised its 'elegant and easy' style but criticized the play for not being realistic enough. Herbert Beerbohm Tree's production in 1901 aimed for a realistic stage picture – even using real grass!

The set design for Beerbohm Tree's 1901 production at His Majesty's Theatre, London. Real grass was used!

DIRECTING
TWELFTH NIGHT

Henry Irving and Beerbohm Tree were actor-managers. They decided how a play should be staged, and played a leading role in it. From the end of the nineteenth century this changed. Productions began increasingly to be organized by a director who guided the actors' understanding of the characters and made decisions about design, costumes and the use of music. The director asked questions about the meaning and atmosphere of the play. They did not act, but observed and guided the growth of a production.

WILLIAM POEL

At the end of the nineteenth century, William Poel founded the English Stage Society. His aim was to get back to the way the Lord Chamberlain's Men and the King's Men would have performed, although it has to be said his actors were less talented.

Norman Wilkinson's geometric design for a 1912 production at the Savoy Theatre, London, directed by Harley Granville-Barker.

In 1897 they took *Twelfth Night* back to the Middle Temple where John Manningham had seen it in 1602. Men at arms stood around the stage, and even in the corridors leading to the hall. The text was spoken quickly, there was almost no set, and actors wore costumes of Shakespeare's time. But the women's parts were played by actresses, not boys as in the sixteenth century.

HARLEY GRANVILLE-BARKER

Poel's rediscoveries about Shakespeare were taken much further in the next few years by Harley Granville-Barker, who directed *Twelfth Night* in 1912. Rather than historical reproduction, Barker tried to find the essential quality of sixteenth-century style. Gardens and rooms were suggested by formal imitation trees or cut-out archways. Costumes expressed character rather than copying old paintings. Above all, the text sounded loud and clear on an uncluttered stage. Barker's *Twelfth Night* began a tradition of Shakespearean production which has dominated the last eighty years.

FINDING ILLYRIA

For Shakespeare and his audience the name 'Illyria' referred to a real place, what we now know as Croatia. The Elizabethans would have heard stories of pirates, wild rioting and drunkenness there. But Shakespeare applies these travellers' tales of a distant land to his own society. Illyria is a sort of upside-down England. In 1993, Ian Judge, directing the play for the RSC, set it in a quite recognizable Stratford-upon-Avon to make this point even more directly. Where is Illyria? It is where the ordinary is turned upside down and the unexpected breaks through.

In his 1987 production for the RSC, Bill Alexander chose to set the play in a sunny Mediterranean village.

WHICH SEASON OF THE YEAR?

A further question for directors is 'what time of year is it?'. Bill Alexander's 1987 RSC production and Bill Buffery's for Orchard Theatre in Devon in 1988, gave the play a summery Mediterranean setting: hot, sun-drenched, whitewashed buildings under blue skies. In contrast, John Caird's 1983 RSC production had an autumnal feel: the set was dominated by a huge English oak tree shedding its leaves. In his 1979 production at Stratford, Terry Hands opened the play in dark winter which turned to spring as love flourished. Kenneth Branagh's 1988 Renaissance Theatre production was set in winter, emphasizing those characters like **Feste** and **Malvolio** who are left out in the cold at the end.

MUSIC IN *TWELFTH NIGHT*

All of Shakespeare's plays contain songs and other music, but in *Twelfth Night* they play a most important part. They create a world of sadness and loss behind the often delighted confusions of the plot. The subtle use of music was used to create a mood. This was made easier for Shakespeare and his company of actors because they increasingly performed indoors – in court and at royal palaces, on tour in market halls or great houses, and eventually in their own purpose-built threatre, the Blackfriars, in London.

Shakespeare was also no doubt encouraged to make much more use of musical effects by the arrival in the acting company of a brilliant clown, Robert Armin, who had a fine singing voice. Armin would have played Feste in the first performances of *Twelfth Night*.

When William Poel tried to recreate *Twelfth Night* at the end of the nineteenth century, he turned to a musician, Arnold Dolmetsch, who was making a name for himself as an expert on early music. This production used sixteenth- and seventeenth-century instruments, such as the lute and recorders, to accompany the songs.

Directors of more recent versions have explored the music in different ways. In Kenneth Branagh's wintery version for the Renaissance Theatre Company, you could hear snatches of 'The Twelve Days of Christmas'. In John Caird's 1983 production at Stratford, the whole company joined in Feste's final song, 'When that I was and a little tiny boy …' In the 1994 RSC production, director Ian Judge wanted music to run through the whole play, sometimes accompanying the spoken text like film music.

Zoe Wanamaker as Viola and Sarah Berger as Olivia in John Caird's RSC production in 1983.

Director Ian Judge rehearsing with Haydn Gwynne (Olivia), Desmond Barrit (Malvolio) and Tony Britton (Sir Toby Belch) at Stratford, 1994.

THE WORLD OF THE PLAY

As well as making decisions about all aspects of a production, a crucial role of a director is to create the world of the play. *Twelfth Night* is full of interesting characters and lovely songs, asks fascinating questions about love and friendship and raises troubling questions about deception and madness. But above all it is a play about a mood. Everything that happens must bring that into focus.

For most directors since Harley Granville-Barker, the mood has been one of joy and delight constantly undercut by a sense of sadness and loss. The play opens sadly: **Viola** thinks her brother has drowned; **Olivia** is mourning the death of her brother. Into this painful world **Sir Toby Belch** and **Maria** burst, full of jollity.

But even they succumb to the sense of time passing, of nothing lasting for ever. Feste's songs about love and loss express this most clearly. For many directors, in fact, his bitter-sweet mood sums it all up:

> *'... pleasure must be paid one time or another.'*

THE MOOD OF LOVE AND LOSS

Directors search for clear ways of showing this mood of love and loss. They may set the play in autumn or winter, when good times are just a fading memory; they may use music to create a suitable atmosphere; they may encourage costume designers to use muted colours – the reds, golds and browns of autumn, or the blacks, whites and greys of winter. Each of these decisions will help actors and audience alike to enter into and respond to the world of the play.

PLAYING MALVOLIO

Whoever first played **Malvolio** for the Lord Chamberlain's Men must have had a lot of fun. But he was also taking a risk interpreting this biting satire on pompous officials. Someone at court might even have recognized himself! It would have been hard to resist the opportunities for comic effect.

Malvolio is a man who is given a little power and authority which goes to his head. He has to be cut down to size. Modern television situation comedy has lots of fun with very similar characters – those in *Red Dwarf* and *The Brittas Empire*, for example; and Captain Mainwaring, the bank manager turned Home Guard Captain in *Dad's Army*, is in some ways a direct descendant of Malvolio the steward.

SELF~CERTAIN

Malvolio is a wickedly accurate picture of the sort of person who is always right. He is so sure of himself that he has no room for any doubt at all. Of course, he sees that as a great strength. He expects to be obeyed by Olivia's servants. He is rude to all those he thinks are less important than himself – and that means most people! He even begins to imagine he is just the sort of person **Olivia** would want to marry.

He convinces himself that as her husband he would be her master.

But the very self-certainty that makes him shout at **Belch**, **Aguecheek** and **Feste** having a late-night drink, also brings about Malvolio's downfall. Having convinced himself that he is perfect in every way, and that Olivia is attracted to him, he is wide open to the trick **Maria** and the others play on him. Because he cannot doubt himself, and has no sense of humour or imagination, he cannot see the obvious practical joke of the letter left lying in the garden. His pride leads him straight into the trap.

DONALD SINDEN

The most satisfying and interesting performances of Malvolio make him more than simply absurdly proud. There are deeper decisions to be made about his character. How much can Malvolio feel anything for others? How far does he suffer, and so how much should we pity him? Donald Sinden, playing the part in 1969, managed to make him both comic and pitiful in his lonely desire to be loved. There is a tradition that Richard Burbage, the actor in Shakespeare's company who first played Hamlet, Othello and King Lear, was the first Malvolio. If that is true, then maybe Shakespeare intended there to be a serious, even tragic, side to the part.

For Sinden, it was very important that Malvolio had no sense of humour. Because he couldn't laugh at others, he couldn't laugh at himself, and because he couldn't laugh at himself, the trick that is played on him destroys him. He is tormented in prison and at the end he leaves Olivia's house, swearing to be revenged. But for Donald Sinden the threat was an empty one. Malvolio's dignity has been shattered. He has nowhere to go, and nothing else to do. When Donald Sinden's Malvolio left the stage, it was to go and kill himself.

A SOCIAL CLIMBER

Actors want to make the most of the ridiculous aspects they find in the character, especially those surrounding Malvolio's social pretensions.

He is a social climber who fantasizes about marrying Olivia because she would be his passport to high status and a life of privilege, which he is sure he deserves.

Laurence Olivier chose to bring out this aspect of Malvolio by giving him a 'posh' accent. In fact decisions about how Malvolio should speak are very important as a way of communicating his social position. Desmond Barritt played him in 1993 using his own accent – Welsh. This made Malvolio an outsider: he would always be isolated because he would always sound different from everyone else. Barritt's performance was richly comic: this Malvolio was a vain man standing on the shifting sands of his own dignity.

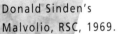

Donald Sinden's Malvolio, RSC, 1969.

Desmond Barritt's Malvolio, RSC, 1994.

PLAYING THE LORDS
(AND LADY) OF MISRULE

In Shakespeare's time, celebrations at Christmas were often led by a Lord of Misrule, whose job was to make sure that the festivities were full of fun and mischief. In *Twelfth Night* this role is taken by **Sir Toby Belch**, **Sir Andrew Aguecheek** and **Maria**. In Ian Judge's 1993 RSC production, Bille Brown played Sir Andrew as a simple clown, entirely innocent and naïve. Brown has played Falstaff and **Malvolio** and believes that 'the magical humour of Shakespeare's comedy is always underscored by bitterness and pain ...' His Aguecheek was both funny and vulnerable, fluttering around Sir Toby one moment, going weak-kneed at the thought of a duel with **Cesario** the next.

Sir Toby Belch (John Thaw),
Sir Andrew Aguecheek (Daniel Massey)
and Feste (Richard O'Callaghan) in
John Caird's 1983 production.

He sums up his experience of the play:

'... the romantic characters become funnier and happier as the play goes on. But those characters who start as comic become exhausted objects of pity. It's as though there are two forces moving in opposite directions in the play'.'

INNOCENCE AND EXPERIENCE

Twelfth Night is a play of youth and age, innocence and experience. The comedy comes from the oldest characters of all, the Lords and Lady of Misrule, and their victim, Malvolio. They all have some connection with **Olivia**: Sir Toby is her uncle, Maria her personal servant, and Sir Andrew thinks he's in love with her. They are all energetic singers, dancers and tricksters, even if Sir Andrew is often a step behind and the object of Maria's and Sir Toby's jokes as well.

But they all go too far and the humour first turns nasty and then simply runs out. Maria is perhaps angry and resentful at Malvolio's attempts to dominate the household and take away her own special relationship with Olivia.

As the steward of Olivia's household, Malvolio is powerful and responsible but definitely a servant. The issue of social position fuels the dislike between him and Sir Toby: 'Art [are you] any more than a steward?' Bill Wallis played Sir Toby in an RSC production in 1991 and brought out some of his less attractive characteristics. This was an ageing, tired, cynical man shamelessly milking Sir Andrew for all the money he could get. Sir Andrew was played by Tim McInnerney as young and painfully gullible.

A Happy Ending?

Twelfth Night is the last day of Christmas, a time when the decorations are finally taken down and life begins to return to normal after the festivities. In *Twelfth Night*, Shakespeare's last real comedy, the mood is always one of time running out and boisterous mischief having to be put away so that real life can take over again. The audience is told that Sir Toby and Maria have been married, though it is hard to believe that their marriage will be as loving or happy as those of Olivia and **Sebastian**, **Viola** and **Orsino**. Sir Andrew, too, goes home a poorer, but probably not much wiser man. Bille Brown is right when he says that the comic characters become 'exhausted objects of pity'.

Abigail McKern (Maria), Richard Briers (Malvolio), Caroline Langrishe (Olivia) and Frances Barber (Viola), in the 1988 Renaissance Theatre production.

VIOLA AND FESTE

Viola is one of several Shakespearean heroines who sets off on an adventure disguised as a boy. The complications of this were far greater for actors and audiences in Shakespeare's time than they are today. Then, there were no professional women actors and all female parts were played by boys. For the boy actor who played Viola, the experience must have been complex. A boy playing a girl playing a boy! It is rather like those sets of Chinese boxes in which opening one reveals another, and so on. What is more, the **Cesario** 'box' attracts the love of another woman, whilst the Viola 'box' is in love with **Orsino**. An actor needs great flexibility and quick-wittedness to be in the right box at the right time!

This challenge has attracted all the greatest actresses. Many accounts of earlier twentieth-century Violas show a search for a thoughtful, even subdued mood. This seems to have been true of Ellen Terry at the turn of the century and of Vivien Leigh in the 1930s. Peggy Ashcroft played Viola twice, in 1938 and 1950. She was praised for her charm and wit on the first occasion, but some felt she lacked sadness on the second. Judi Dench played Viola with great success in 1969.

The interplay of liveliness and sadness in her performance was one of its most remarkable, and satisfying, features.

A performance by Dorothy Tutin at Stratford in 1958 captured the many moods of the character very well. Critics praised her as,

'the absolute Viola, all gentleness, courage, steadfastness and fear.'

Viola/Cesario (Dorothy Tutin) reunited with her twin brother Sebastian (Ian Holm) in Peter Hall's production in 1958.

PLAYING FESTE

Robert Armin, the first actor to play **Feste**, was a singer and musician and a witty performer of comic roles. He was also the first Fool in *King Lear* a few years later. Like Feste, that Fool is an 'allowed fool' too: a court jester; a funny man with a licence to tell the truth, however painful; a man who keeps his wits when everyone around him is losing theirs. This is Feste's job, and it makes many demands on any actor who plays the role.

The importance of casting the right actor for the part is crucial. He must be able to sing and to act across a wide range of moods. Max Adrian played a worldly-wise, rather bitter Feste in Peter Hall's production in 1958. He delivered his songs sarcastically. By contrast in 1993 at Stratford, Derek Griffiths, with his fine singing voice, began from Feste's musical skill. Part of this Feste's isolation was the fact that he was an artist, only really able to express himself through music.

Anton Lesser played Feste in the Renaissance Theatre production in 1988, and fortunately his performance was recorded on video-tape. He was a man clinging on to sanity; only being a fool seemed to stop him from going mad in this topsy-turvy world (just like Lear's Fool). He arrived at **Olivia's** house in a snowstorm carrying a suitcase. The audience was left in no doubt that this Feste loved Olivia, one of the loves in the play which is never returned. At the end he left Illyria once more. He sang his song, picked up his suitcase and left the stage in the snow, closing the gate of Olivia's garden behind him. The winter revels were over and new starts had to be made. The happiness of the loving couples at the end of this production was cut across by the sadness of those who remained alone, still searching for the 'other half' to make them whole.

Anton Lesser was a sad and lonely Feste in the wintery Renaissance Theatre production in 1988.

INDEX